日本建築の形と空間

NORMAN F. CARVER, JR.

東京・彰国社刊・一九五五

JAPANESE

photographs by

FORM and
SPACE
of
ARCHITECTURE

NORMAN F. CARVER, JR.

SHOKOKUSHA tokyo

book designed by the author

published by

SHOKOKUSHA PUBLISHING CO.

2–11 Hirakawa-cho
Chiyoda-ku
Tokyo, Japan

CONTENTS

目 次

preface

From the many hundreds of photographs which I took during two years' study in Japan (1953—55) the 158 included in this book have been chosen. In the selection of the photographs and in the accompanying commentary no attempt has been made to cover the whole sweep of Japanese architectural history or to present a complete description of its materials and techniques. Meticulous cataloguing of influence and counter-influence, careful tabulation of plan and measured facade, as useful as they are, too often have failed to convey any real meaning of Japanese architecture. I have assumed, therefore, some basic acquaintance with Japanese architecture on the part of the reader and proceeded above and beyond these particulars to define the general organization of Japanese architectural design and its implications for modern architecture. Such an approach, of course, is concerned not with fact alone but with interpretation of fact. And it creates the difficult problem of communicating the subtle essences of three dimensional form and space through the two dimensional medium of the printed page. In an attempt to minimize this barrier to understanding I have restricted my written commentary and relied primarily on the uninterrupted flow of visual images, interpretative in their own right, to recreate the particular atmosphere of Japanese architecture.

In the creation of this book I owe a great deal to all the many persons and institutions that gave me assistance during my stay in Japan: first, to the Fulbright Commission for awarding me the original study grant and to the Fulbright staff—especially Mrs. Etsu Nakagawa of Kyoto for her unceasing help; to the students and teachers of Kyoto University, particularly Professor Jiro Murata, for their guidance to the best architecture; to the Imperial Household Office in Kyoto for granting permission to photograph the great buildings in their charge; to the many anonymous and friendly farm families, priests of innumerable temples and shrines with whom we shared a cup of tea; to Priest Hagiwara of the Ise Grand Shrine; to my good friend Yojiro Yoshimura of Osaka who was so generous in showing his beautiful house; to Miss Chieko Kuno for really starting the whole project on its way and to the whole Kuno family for their friendship and their inestimable help; to Yoshihisa Miyauchi of the publishers staff and Ryuichi Hamaguchi, who has done the translation, for their initial interest, friendly advice and encouragement; but particularly to my wife, fellow architect and constant companion, for her unfailing enthusiasm and faith. To her this book is affectionately dedicated.

Kyoto, August, 1955 N. F. C.

たフルブライト委員会およびそのスタッフの方方、とくに京都の中川えつ子夫人の変らざる援助に対して、また、すぐれた建築への導きをしてくださった京都大学の教授および学生諸氏、とくに村田治郎教授、貴重な建物の写真を撮ることを許してくださった宮内庁の京都事務所、親切な農家の家族の人々、伊勢神宮の萩原宮司、その所有にかかる美しい邸宅を親切にみせてくださった私のよき友、大阪の吉村要治郎氏、私の計画の出発と進行に対して厚い友情と測りきれぬ援助を与えてくださった久能ちえ子さんとそのご家族、編集者の宮内嘉久氏および翻訳にあたった浜口隆一氏の本書に対する友情ある助言と励まし、そして最後に、つねによき伴侶であり協力建築家でもある私の妻の、本書に対する変らざる熱意と信頼に対して、彼女にこの本を心から捧げる。

6

はじめに

この本に収められた一五八枚の写真は、私の日本留学（一九五三─五五）の二年間に撮影した数千枚の中から選んだものです。写真の選択とその解説にあたっては、日本の建築史の全貌を伝えるとか、日本建築の技法や材料についての詳しい解説をするとかは意図しておりません。

平面や立面の、実測した様式の史的一覧表とか、影響したり、されたりした細かい図面とか、それはそれとして有益なものに違いありませんが、日本建築の本当の意味を正しく伝えることには失敗することが多いようです。そうした理由から、本書では読者の側に日本建築についての或る程度の基礎知識を予想し、細かな点はいちおう離れて、日本建築のデザインにみられる普遍的構成や近代建築に対するそれの含蓄といったものを掴みだすことに努めました。このような試みにあって、問題になってくるのは当然、単に事実だけではなく、事実に対する解釈ないし理解であります。また三次元にわたる形と空間の微妙な内容を、印刷されたページという二次元の媒体によって伝達しなければならない難問題もおきてきます。この制約を最少限にくい止めるために、私は文字による解説をなるべく減らして、視覚像の連続的な流れをつくりだすことによって日本建築の独特な雰囲気を再現させようとしました。

日本滞在中の私に与えられた多くの方々の援助なしにはこの本は生れなかったことでしょう。

まず第一に、日本留学の奨学金を私に与えられ

7

introduction

Inevitably, an individual confronted by a new situation searches for some guide to action, first in his own past experience and then in the experience of others. This is the natural course of the intellect and it enables new and complex situations to be met by building on the collective accomplishments of Man. Strong similarities may even extend this search across the boundaries of space and time to other cultures. Such an inter-cultural affinity exists today between modern architecture and ancient Japanese architecture; for out of an analogous attitude toward the problems of architecture have evolved forms and structural methods of striking resemblance. This means Japanese architecture with its mastery of the fundamentals of form and space is an "experience" of great significance for the modern architect. Furthermore, even as one of history's most highly developed and thoroughly integrated styles, over the fifteen centuries of its growth, Japanese architecture has been able to absorb vital changes in form, materials, and philosophy and yet maintain its essential integrity. Such a continuity of growth and change, free from stifling arbitrary doctrine, is a basic aim of modern architecture. But its accomplishment necessitates a definition of certain broad yet fundamental principles of architecture—the need to find in architecture those abstractions that approach the essence, "the felt structure of reality".

The present book, therefore, is a selection of the forms and spaces of Japanese architecture that have seemed to me, as a modern architect, particularly valuable in shaping these definitions; that is, their meaning to modern architecture transcends simple resemblance to illuminate some universal truth in the world of architecture. Of all the fundamental principles discoverable in Japanese architecture the most sweeping and at the same time the most profound is a pervasive sense of order —a precise organization of the architecture that extends almost effortlessly to a breadth and depth of control, welding together the inherent patterns of form and space into a unique organic whole. It is this revelation of an all embracing but innately mutable order that is perhaps the most important lesson of Japanese architecture to the modern world. For man gradually has come to realize that visual order and its intellectual manifestations are not merely pleasant adjuncts to civilization, but vital to the existence of Man and Society.

We now understand that the existence of order in the universe is a precarious and artificial state. Recent physics has confirmed that all matter tends always to move towards the simplest state (thermodynamic equilibrium) or disorder. Entropy is the measurement of this tendency and maximum entropy, its final consequence, would find all matter completely homogeneous, orderless, and totally formless. The form, the order of life, therefore, is merely a temporary and local reversal of this universal tendency to disorder. Life is constantly being encroached upon and must constantly take in order to maintain its existence. Human vision is one important means by which order is taken into the life system, but since entropy is a universal tendency, it also operates within the mind so that all vision moves toward homogeneity and rest Such a state is delayed. however, by the visual comprehension of external order—the influx of external light energy · which comes to us as information......or negative entropy; that is, it imparts order or form". This external light energy originates in the visual environment and the dominance of architecture in this environment makes it the most potentially effective stimulation to order over which man exercises control. For architecture can have not only the immediate impact of primary geometry, but. moreover, the long range effect of penetration beyond surface configuration and its constant revelation of deep-seated order.

These photographs, then, try to portray a feeling for the whole of Japanese architecture in terms of its visual order of form and space. They cover a wide scope in space and time, linking the palaces. the common houses of the city and farm. the tea houses, the temples, and the shrines, all of which by their strong mutual influence have contributed to the total feeling. Consideration of the whole from the two primary aspects of space and form makes it possible to clarify the essential order of each, but as forms exist only in space and space is always defined and directed by form, in the concept of one the other is always implied.

Even though photographs cannot substitute for the actual experience of Japanese architecture certain advantages lie within photography's limitations. In its ability to record only a small segment of the total impression is the advantage in abbreviating to the point of clarity—in pointing out and intensifying the essentials of any impression. Moreover. very few single buildings or building complexes exist today in sufficiently good condition and purity to convey these essentials as a whole, and fragments from all facets must contribute to establishing a sense of the whole. Thus there may appear to be a concentration upon detail but the organization of the book will make evident the interrelationship of these details. and further, point out by this attention the contributing order of detail. how the ordering of parts gives form to the whole—one thing that modern architecture in its haste to evolve its own "significant forms" has usually overlooked.

Appreciation of Japanese architecture in the abstract—in photographs devoid of a sense of function and cultural relationship—is possible only because the powerful order of its primary geometry imposes its own articulation on the observer and the mind first reacts to these forms in space and to the energies and tensions generated by their relationships Appreciation is heightened. however, by further study that brings the gradual realization that this architecture had an intrinsic functional, cultural basis—that the individual building was part of a wider pattern and that this pattern was shaped by the way of life which it contained and instrumented.

ゆくことは宇宙の普遍的傾向であるから、視覚もまた、均質性と静止へと向う傾向の中で働らくことになる。しかし、そうした状態は外界の秩序に対する視覚的な理解——すなわち外界から報知（インフォーメイション）として流れこんでくる光のエネルギーあるいは負のエントロピー（それは秩序ないし形を伝達する）——によって遅らされる。こうした外界からのエネルギーは視覚的環境から発生する。そしてこの環境を建築が支配しているならば、そこから出てくる光のエネルギーは生命に内在的な秩序に対して永続的、もっとも効果的な刺戟体となる。建築は人間の心に対して初等幾何学的な直接衝撃をもちうるだけでなく、さらに表面的な外観をこえて、内部へと滲透する永続的な効果と深く根ざした秩序の永続的な表現をもちうるものなのである。

ここに集められた写真は、こうした意味において日本建築の全体にわたり、その形と空間の視覚的秩序についての一人の建築家の感じを試みたものである。それらは宮殿、町家、農家、茶室、寺院、神社等きわめて広く地理と歴史を包含しており、これら相互間の強い関連はあい寄って全体としての感じをかもしだすように努めている。ここにしたように、全体を空間と形という二つの基本局面に分けることは、それぞれに内在する秩序を明確にするためにはよい方法ではあるけれども、もともと形は空間の中でのみ存在するものだし、空間はつねに形によって限定されるか方向づけられるかしているものだから、互いに他を含みあっているものだということを忘れるわけにはいかない。

写真で日本建築についての本当の鑑賞体験に代えることはもちろんできないけれども、写真にはその限界の範囲内で若干の長所もある。写真のもつ性能の一つ——全体の印象のごく限られた視野だけを、しかし精細に記録するという性能は、その切り捨て作用によって問題を明確にさせ、印象における本質的なものだけを指摘し、強調するのに有効である。さらにまた、これらの本質的なものを伝えるべく、全体として純粋かつ良好な状態を保っているような建物が、もはやごくすこししか残っていない今日では、可能なあらゆるところから、断片的なものでもすべて集めてくることは、全体の感じをつくりだすのに役立つのである。かくて、本書の写真は建築の部分の部分（ディテール）にもっぱら集中することになる。しかしこの本全体としての構成は、これらの部分同志の相互関係を明瞭なものとし、さらに部分が貢献しているところの秩序——いかにして部分の秩序が全体に形（フォーム）を賦与するかということを明らかにしてくれるであろう。それは近代建築の、自己の〝独自の形〟を発展させるのに急いできたあまり、ともすれば見逃してきたものである。

日本建築をこのような抽象のうちにみる——機能や文化との関連を考えずに写真を通して鑑賞する、ということを可能にするのは、日本建築の幾何学的な力強い秩序が、観る者に対してその構成を強くひき起される印象づけるからであり、また空間におけるそれらの形、さらにそれら相互の関係によってひき起される緊張感とエネルギーに対して、観る者の心が第一に反応するからにほかならない。とはいえ、日本建築についての研究を深めて、そこに内在する機能的・文化的な基礎、さらに個々の建物が包みながら奉仕する日本人の生活様式によって生みだされたものだということを理解することは、日本建築の鑑賞をいっそう高めるものであることはいうまでもない。

一部分である広汎な文化型を知り、そしてこの文化型は、これらの建物が包みながら奉仕する日本人

序　説

はじめてぶつかる新しい状況に当面したばあい、ひとはまず最初に自身の過去の経験を振りかえり、ついで他の人々の経験について調べてゆこうとするものである。それは智慧のある者の当然なやり方であり、新しい複雑な条件に対して、人間がその経験の集合と蓄積に基いて立ち向ってゆくことを得させる方法である。これとよく似たことは、個人についてだけでなく、文化についても国境や歴史を超えていえるのではあるまいか。このような文化の相互的な親近性、いわば合い性といったものが、今日、近代建築と古い日本建築とのあいだに存在している。というのは、両者は建築の当然な課題に対する相似した態度から、驚くほどよく似た構造的な手法を展開させているからである。つまり形（フォーム）と空間（スペース）の根本をしっかりと把えている日本建築は、近代建築にとって意義深い "経験の宝庫" なのである。世界の建築史上もっとも高度に精練された様式の一つとして、日本建築はその千五百年にわたる史的展開において、形や材料や哲学の変遷を敏感に経験しながらも、しかもその本質的な統合性はつねに保ちつづけてきた。窒息しそうな専断的教義に凝り固まってしまうことなく、こうした発展と変化の連続性をもちつづけること――これこそ近代建築の基本的目標である。しかし近代建築が成熟しつづけてゆくためには、幅があって、しかも根ざすところ深い建築の諸原理を明確にしてゆくことが必要である。すなわち "真実さ（レアリティ）を感得した構造" という、建築の精髄に迫る抽象作用をしっかりと把えることが必要である。

この本は、こうした考え方にもとづいて、一人の近代建築家としての私が、日本建築の形と空間から特に重要だと思われるものを選びだしたものである。つまり、近代建築に対してこれらのものが単なる表面上の類似をもつというだけでなく、その意義において建築の普遍的な真実を照しだすよう に、と選ばれている。日本建築にみられる基本的諸原理のうちで、もっとも一般的で、しかも最も深いものは秩序（オーダー）についての感覚であり、それは日本建築のあらゆるところに滲みこんでいる。すなわち建築の全面に拡がって、その形と空間のすべての部分を融けあわせ、建築をひとつのユニィクで有機的な全体へとまとめてゆく、的確な総合性である。すべてのものを包みながら、しかも内在的な変化に富む秩序の表現こそ、日本建築が近代の世界に贈るもっとも貴重な教えであろう。われわれは視覚的な秩序とその知的表現というものが、文化にとっての単に楽しげな装飾といったものではなくて、人間と社会の生存にとって根ざすところ深い生命的なものだということを、だんだんに認識するようになってきている。

今日われわれは、宇宙における秩序というものの存在が、不安定で人工的な状態なのだということを知っている。最近の物理学の確認するところによれば、宇宙のあらゆる事象はもっとも単純な状態（熱力学的な平衡状態）または秩序の消失した状態へと向ってつねに動いてゆく。こうした傾向を数量的に示すのがエントロピー（熱力学的静止函数）であるが、このエントロピーが増大してゆく状態の結果は、あらゆる事象の完全な等質、秩序の消失、すなわち形が完全に消滅してしまう状態である。したがって、形すなわち生命の秩序は、こうした無秩序的絶対静止の状態へ向う宇宙全体の傾向の、一時的にしてかつ部分的な反逆にすぎない。生命はつねにおびやかされているものであり、その存在をつづけてゆくためには秩序を保ちつづけてゆかなければならない。人間の視覚は生命体に秩序をもってゆくためのもっとも重要な手段の一つである。とはいえエントロピー（静止函数）が増加してその存在

11

FORM

OF JAPANESE

ARCHITECTURE

The concept of form in architecture embraces more than simply exterior shape or configuration; rather, it includes the principle by which a building exists—that organic unity given by the intrinsic harmony of all its elements. It encompasses all aspects of spatial form, from visible shape to internal structure as they are ordered into a coherent whole. When considered in this sense of inherent harmony and order, the forms of Japanese architecture are a stimulating experience for modern architects. For by this degree of abstraction it is possible to move beyond particular shapes with their inseparable cultural and emotional associations into the area of fundamental relationships and principles of order. Japanese architectural form, to be fully relevant across the boundaries of time and culture, must be seen primarily in this way—as a highly ordered series of relationships in space and time.

Order implies the dominance of some unifying concept which relates the complex elements of architecture in some meaningful way. In a broad sense this may be accomplished by the absolute relationships of a static, geometrical symmetry to which the form of most Japanese religious and official buildings adheres. But the unique contribution of Japanese architecture has been the development of a system of asymmetrical order, the inherent energy of which multiplied its effectiveness as negative entropy, or order. For asymmetry imparts a unique vitality by requiring participation in experience; by suggestion, in directing the mind to complete the incomplete, by providing a constant source of ever changing relationships in space. Asymmetrical order is not an externally imposed finality but an extension of the process of life. It recognizes that life is not static, perfectable, finalized, but rather that its essence is growth, change, and relatedness

The larger asymmetrical order of Japanese architecture found its motivation in the free structural network that enclosed the various unsymmetrical functional requirements. This network determined a rectangular geometry which the clarity of the structure transmitted throughout the whole, exerting a rhythmic influence on all elements of the composition. Thus, expression of structure established an integral geometric order, asymmetrical in nature, that not only determined the broad organization of total form, but also penetrated deeply into the architecture to create a formal unity even to the smallest detail. This unity was further expanded by the harmony of colors and textures originating in the generic compatability of natural materials. The consequence was an architecture meaningful in Japanese life and an honest expression of a civilization's "impulse to form".

形

建築における形（フォーム）という概念は単なる外観や形状というだけでなく、それ以上のもの、すなわちある一つの建物を存在させている原理——建物のすべての要素を貫いて内在する調和と有機的な統一を含んでいる。形（フォーム）は直接眼にみえる形態（シェイプ）から内部の構造にいたるあらゆるものを含み、それらを脈絡ある一つの全体にまとめているものである。この意味での内在的な調和と秩序についてみてゆくと、日本建築にとって示唆するところ深い、すばらしい体験である。なぜなら、こうした抽象作業を通せば日本建築の文化的・感情的な連想を伴った、一つ一つの、あの形態この形態といったものを超えて、基本的な関係と秩序の原理の領域へと入ってゆくことができるからである。日本建築は文化と歴史の制約を超えて、世界の現代建築家にとって空間と時間におけるすぐれた秩序の連続体としてみられるに値いするものである。

秩序とは建築の複雑な諸要素をひとつの意味あるものにまとめてゆく、なにかある統一的な構想の支配を意味する。広い意味では、それは静的で幾何学的な左右対称（シンメトリー）によって達成されているといえるかもしれない。事実、日本の宗教的および公共的な建築の多くのものは厳格なシンメトリーになっている。しかし、日本建築のユニークな貢献は、非対称の秩序、すなわちエントロピー（熱力学的静止函数）の反対のものとして、効果を倍加させる内的エネルギーにある。非対称な建築は対称な建築とちがい、鑑賞するにあたって人間がそれに参加することを要求し、見る人間の心に対して不完全なところを補って完結させるように暗示する。すなわち、空間における関係位置の絶えざる変化を生みだしてゆく源泉となることによって、建築の生気（ヴァイタリティ）を人間の心に伝達するものである。非対称な秩序は外面に現われた完結性ではなくて、生命の流れの展開である。それは、生命が静止的・完結的・終止的なものでなく、その本質が生長・変化・相互連関であることを認識する。

日本建築に、この広汎にわたる非対称的秩序をもたらす動因は、さまざまの非対称な機能的な要求をつつむ構造組織の自由な構成にある。この構造組織は各部分の構成に律動的な影響を及ぼしながら、建物の全体にわたって構造の明快さを伝達してゆく幾何学的矩形性を決定する。かくて構造の表現は緻密な幾何学的かつ非対称的な秩序を完成する。それは全体の形の有機性を決定するばかりでなく、ごく小さな細部にいたるまでの形態的統一感をつくりだすものとして、建築に奥深く滲透しているものである。この統一感は自然のままの素材に特有な性質にもとづく色彩と肌理（テクスチュア）の調和によって、さらに拡げられる。こうして創りだされたものは日本人の生活に意義ふかい一つの建築であり、或る一つの文化の〝形についての鼓動〟とでもいうべき、生き生きとした正直な表現である。

15

A long history of primitive contact with nature developed in the Japanese a profound respect for natural form; in it they found evidence of a larger order to which they felt inexorably linked. And the natural, organic way became to them the religious and right way.

自然に対する素朴な結びつきの永い歴史は・日本人の心の中に自然の形に対する深い尊敬心をはぐくんだ。日本人は自然の中にある偉大な秩序をみいだし、その秩序の中に彼ら自身、動きのとれぬほど、しっかりと結びつけられていると感じている。自然な、有機的な方法は日本人にとって宗教的・倫理的なものとなった。

8

……そして人間と自
然との依存関係、お
よびさまざまな形の
あいだの相互関連に
ついての感覚──し
かも人間の心と手に
よって鍛えられた本
質的なコントラスト。

....and an innate sense of the interdependence of man and
nature and the forms of each—yet the essential contrast wrought
by the mind and hand of man.

11

A simple direct structure was the basis for the evolving forms. Such structure was understandable and relatable to a common experience with the fundamental forces involved. As skill increased, these multiple forces eventually were resolved into their vertical and horizontal components thereby creating the basic rectangular geometrical order of post and beam structure. The underlying order was thus not an arbitrarily imposed geometry but structurally derived and contributing to the functioning unity of the whole.

12

展開してゆく形の基礎は単純で直接的な構造であった。こうした構造は理解されやすいものであり、かつ、そこに含まれている基礎的な力学についての普通の経験と結びついたものであった。技術と熟練が増すにつれて、これらの複雑な諸力は垂直と水平の成分に還元されつくし、それによって柱と梁による構造方式の幾何学的な直角の基本的秩序がつくりだされた。基本となる秩序は、だから恣意的におしつけられた幾何学でなくて、構造的に根拠をもつものであり、建物全体の機能的統一に寄与するものであった。

建築的な要求が複雑になり、技術が高度になっていっても、構造的な組織の明快さは空間における広汎な相互連関のスケールを確保しつづけた。

In the growing complexity of building requirements and with the refinement of techniques the clarity of the structural fabric maintained the scale of the wider relationships in space.

しかし構造的事実を単に示すとい
うことが最後の目的なのではなか
った。日本人は〝形（フォーム）
という考え方が本質的に型（パタ
ン――繰り返してゆく形）を作る
ことであり型を選ぶ機能である〟
ということを感じていた。そして
空間的な形の構造的必要は次第に
一連の型に変ってゆき、そして全
体の動的な秩序をつくりだすリズ
ムを放射することととなった。

But the mere statement of structural fact was not the final intent. The Japanese sensed that "the perception of form is essentially a pattern making, pattern selecting function" and the structural necessities of spatial form were gradually transformed into a series of patterns and radiating rhythms that created a dynamic order of the whole.

17

18

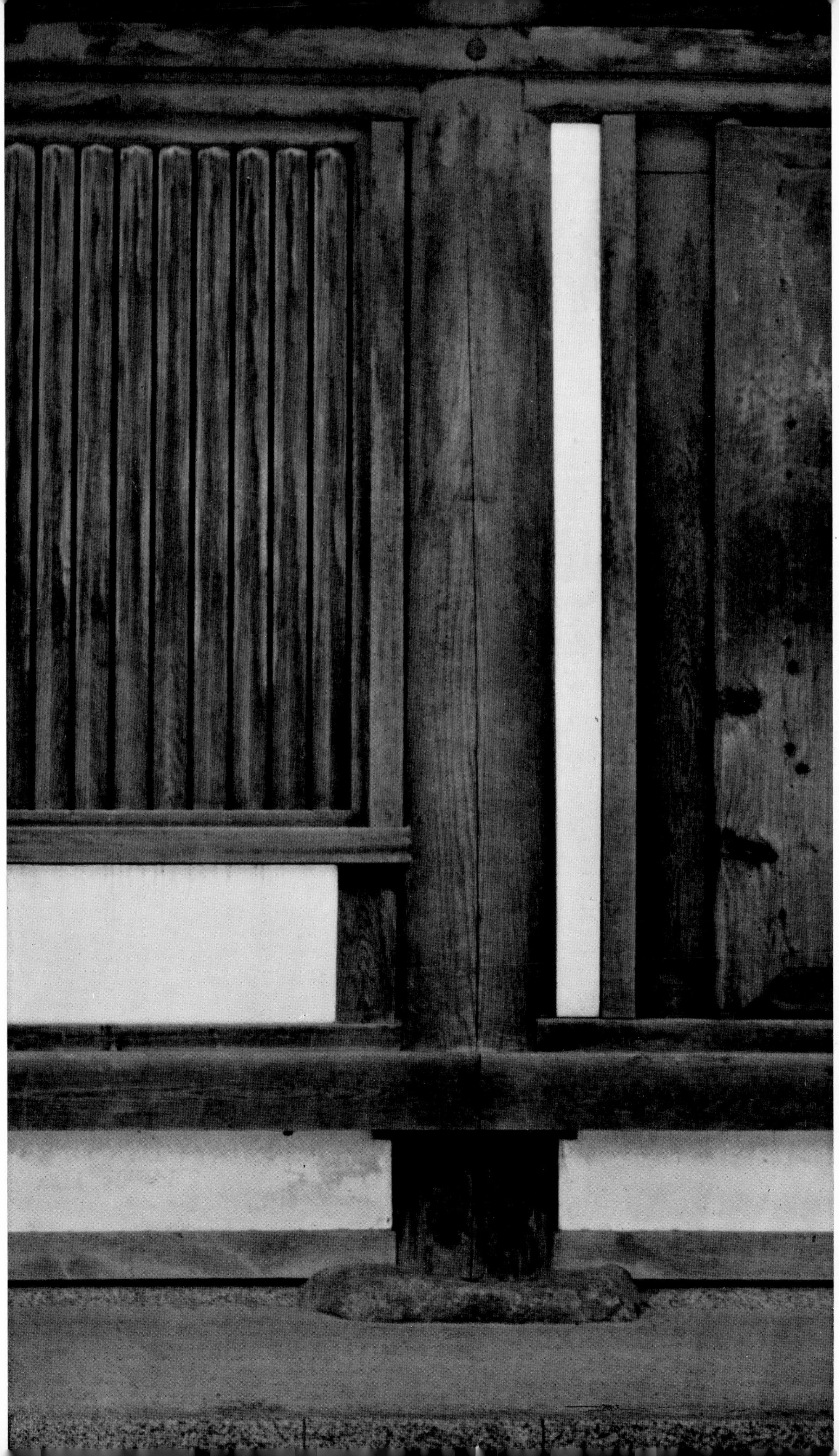

◀26

27

対照的な素材や要素や力を交叉させて
並べてゆくことは、表現の生きた源で
あった。こういう、一見したところで
はごくありふれた建築的事象の中に、
普遍的な秩序が相関関係の表現の深い
感じを与えられているのである。暗色
の強い柱と白く薄い壁は、支持体と非
支持体というそれらのもつ真の意味を
表現する。個々の要素、個々の素材は
それぞれの存在をはっきりと主張して
いるが、それと同時にそれ自身を超え
た、より高い価値をつくりだす──素
材から発する精神的な価値、普遍的な
ものの個における発現。

The conjunction of contrasting materials, elements, or forces was a vital source of expression. Here in these seemingly mundane events of architecture the overall order was given the added depth of expressive relationships The strong dark column and the thin white wall convey their true meanings of support and non-support. Each element, each material has its own existence stated clearly yet always with a sense of value beyond itself — of the spiritual emmanating trom the material and the universal reflected in the particular.

29

28

35

45

46

機能的な諸要素――窓・扉・垣根・格子――は、構造的なリズムを小さいスケールで繰り返しながら、微妙な対位法的魅力を全体の大きな構造の脈動に対して加えている。これらの格子は町家を街路からまもるのに役立ち、時として幾層もの面に重なりあいながら、リズミックなにぎやかさをつくりだしている。

The functional elements—windows. doors, fences, and grills—still reflecting the structural rhythms in a reduced scale add a delicate counterpoint to the heavy structural beat. The grills serve to shield city houses from the street and often occur in several planes achieving a rhythmic complexity.

47

58283

50

51

53

自然のままの色とテクスチュアに対する強い好みは、自然と建築との連続性を作りだすのにつねに役立っている。さらにテクスチュアは、建物のスケールを掴むための重要な手がかりの一つとなり、また近寄ってみたときに深みのある視覚的なおもしろさを加える。

The insistence on natural finish—color and texture—serves always to establish the continuity from nature to architecture. Texture, moreover, provides one of the basic clues to scale and the added depth of close range visual interest.

55

58

61

Natural color and texture and the dominate structural module 5ify these various rhythms, textures, and shapes into a single composition. But in the creation of the whole, structure is not always honest, evident and logical. Apparent structural members are freely added for their rhythmic decorative effect and others such as diagonal bracing carefully hidden. This is the mature handling of structure by men sensitive to the effect on the whole of each of its parts.

自然のままの色とテクスチュアおよび構造を貫くモデュールは、これらのさ
まざまなリズムとテクスチュアと形を一つの単純明快なコンポジションに統
一する。しかし全体の建物の創造においては、必ずしもつねに正直であり倫
理的であるとは限らない。構造的のようにみえる部材が、リズミカルな装飾
的な効果のために自由につけ加えられたり、また構造的に有用なはずの対角
線の筋違いは、意識的にかくされる。こうしたことは、おのおのの部分の全
体に対する効果について、敏感な人間による〝大人の〟取り扱いかたとでも
いうべきか。

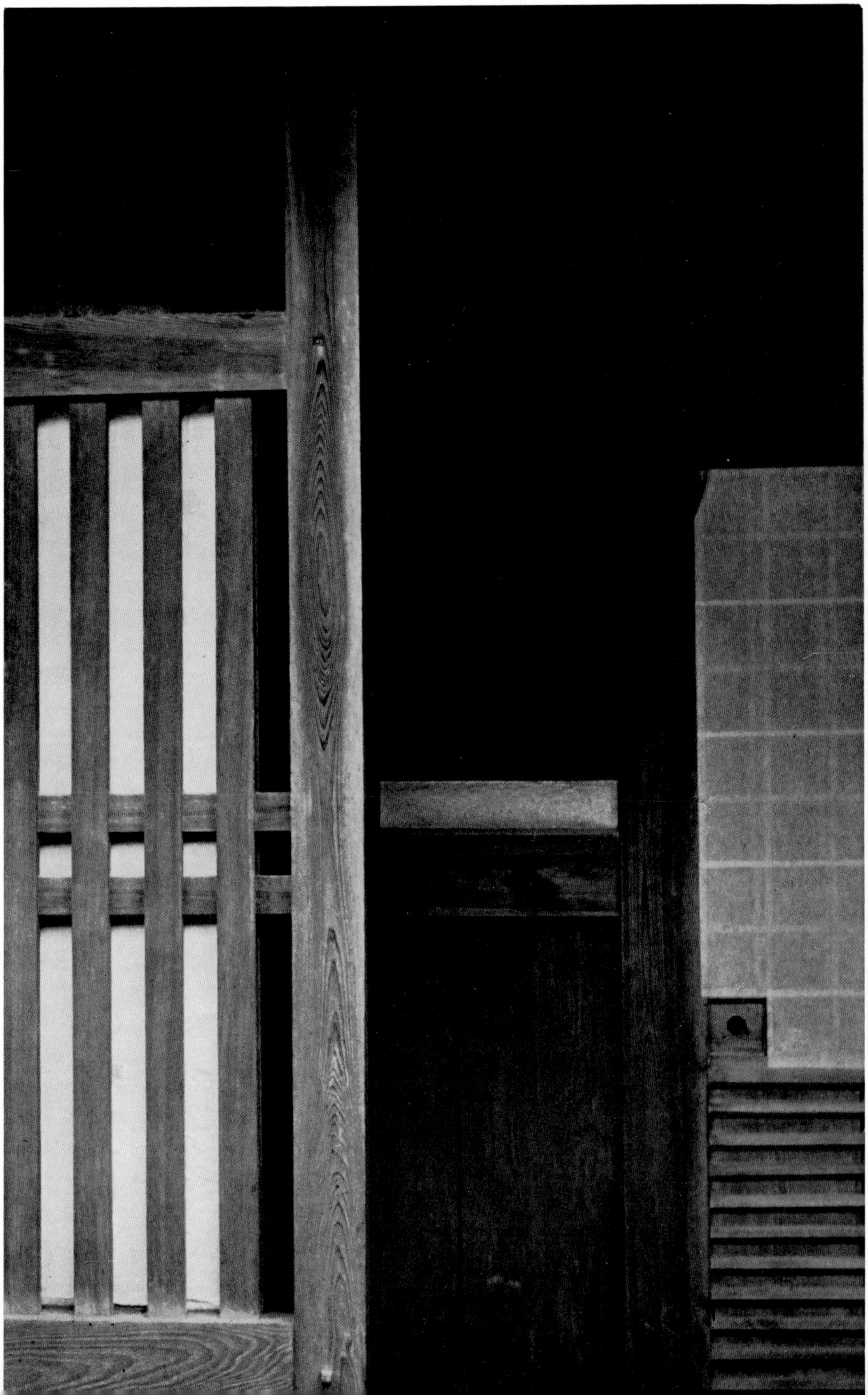

The intricate patterns are contained between the powerful horizontals of the roof and the earth. The roof in Japanese architecture is the most difficult element to relate in the composition. It, of course, provides that dominance of one element which helps to unify the total form, but more important it acts in the visual sense as a separate element serving in an abstract way to divide the small scale events beneath from the background; its hovering dominance implies a felt limit to the architecture as shelter, at the same time permitting a freedom of movement beneath.

こうした複雑にいりくんだ形（パターン）は、屋根と地面の力強い水平線のあいだにおさめられる。屋根は日本の建築のコンポジションにおいて、説明するのにもっともむずかしい要素である。それはもちろん全体の形を統一させるのに効果のある支配的要素の一つである。しかし屋根はまた視覚的な意味において、さらにその下の小さなスケールの諸物を背景から切り離すように働く。空にかかる屋根の優越性は覆い（シェルター）として、しかもその下のものに自由な運動を許すようなものとして、建築の感覚的な限界を意味している。

77

吉村邸。最近修復されたものだが、四百年前に建てられた豪農の邸宅は、日本建築の形と空間のみごとな実例である。構造を貫く秩序は明確であって、線と面の交錯——床の畳、半透明な障子、純白な襖など——は、構造の規則正しいリズムによって、屋根の下に出たり入ったり動きながら連なりあう幾つかの面と一緒になって、いつ見ても新しい形（パターン）と相互関係をつくりだす。

The recently restored house of Mr. Yoshimura, a four hundred year old aristocratic farm house is a superb example of Japanese architectural form and space. The pervading order of structure is strongly evident and the interplay of lines and planes—the tatami of the floor, the translucent shoji, and the brilliant white fusuma doors is integrated by this regular structural rhythm into a series of planes that move in and out under the roof in ever new patterns and relationships.

87

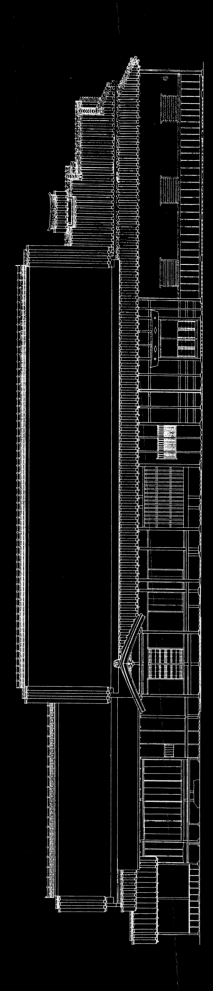

YOSHIMURA-TEI front elevation

吉村邸・正面図

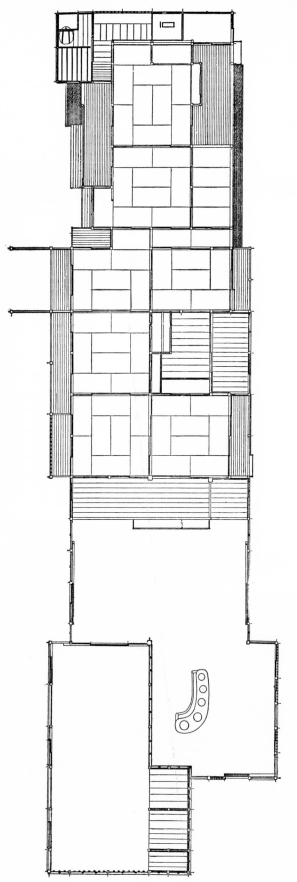

N

吉村邸（右）見上図（左）平面図

YOSHIMURA-TEI

◀ Plan

Structure (Reflected Plan) ▶

0 1   5   10   20   ft

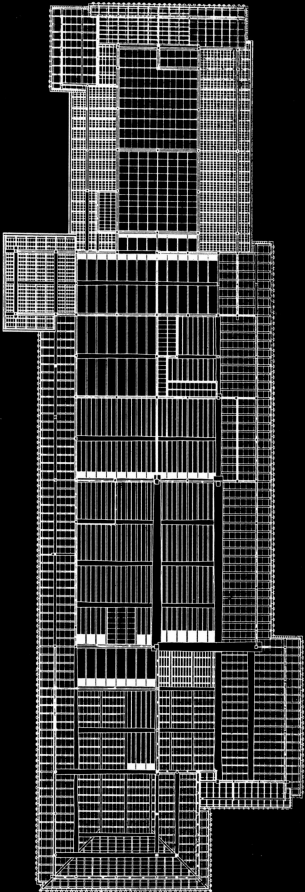

94 ▶

95

手段・態度・精神の共通公分母（コモン・デノミネーター）は、建築の大らかな方向を決定する有機的な統一を意味すると同時に多様な自然的エネルギーに協力する。統一された構造のモデュールの枠の中で、個人個人の試みによって進められる成長と変化の連続性。

A common denominator of means, attitudes, and spirit meant an organic unity defining the broad direction of architecture while incorporating the natural energy of diversity; continuity of growth and change stimulated by individual experimentation within the framework of a unified structural module.

97

98

The same innate sense of form creating the rich interplay between the
pattern of architecture and the landscape ·····

この同じ天賦の造形感覚は、建築と風景とのあいだに豊かな相互貫通を創りだす……

SPACE

OF JAPANESE

ARCHITECTURE

Transcending defining forms and materials, the abstract space of Japanese architecture is a rich source of experience for modern architects. Though it parallels remarkably the modern perception of space, the Japanese attitude toward space, unlike the modern, is inherent in their deep rapport with nature. Chinese Zen Buddhism, also, on its arrival in Japan found a concept of reality similar to its own. It was this similarity between naive understanding and a sophisticated doctrine that resulted in Zen's extensive influence on Japanese art and life. In Japanese art space assumed a dominant role and their attitude toward it was strengthened by two important Zen concepts. Zen affirmed the reality of immediate experience and yet declared its indivisibility from a present defined as "the moving infinity"—its oneness with life in eternal flux. Space was felt to be the only true essential for only in space was movement possible. Space was the universal medium through which life moved in constant transformation, in which place and time were only relative states. Change was something that could not be arrested but only guided—a movement through space that could not be confined but only directed. Such vast concepts underlying the approach to Japanese architecture might have prompted an overwhelming scale. Rather, it developed in the Japanese a concern for the small, human scale events in architecture and a realization of the need to progressively relate these to the greater whole. The stress was on continuity of relationships—the ordered progression of Man's movement through time and space. Architecture defined the individual's relationships to this spatial-temporal continuity by its rhythmic extension from the near and definite to the distant and indefinable.

In Japanese architecture the extension of these three-dimensional relationships was by an asymmetrical order which gave the feeling of infinite extendability. Based on this order the architecture developed within and beyond the structural cage as a series of patterns and planes of reference precisely defining certain portions of continuous space.

130

空　間

日本建築の抽象的な空間は、限定された形と素材を超えて、近代建築家にとって学ぶところ多い源泉である。日本人の空間概念は、近代の空間概念とよく似てはいるけれども、それと違って、自然に対する日本人の深い親和性にもとづいたものである。禅がシナから日本に渡ってきたとき、日本人のこの生得の対自然感情が禅のそれとよく似ていることを見いだした。日本の芸術と生活に禅があのように広く深い影響を及ぼすことになったのも、こうした自然への素朴な理解と禅の洗練された教義とのあいだに深い類似性があったからである。日本の芸術において空間というものは重大な役割をもっているが、空間に対するそうした態度は禅の二つの主要な概念によって裏づけられ、いっそう強められた。禅は直接的体験の真実性を否定はしないが、しかし〝流動してゆく無限〟として定義される現在──永遠な流れにおける生命とともにある一者──の非分割性を強く語る。空間は生命が絶えず変化しながら動いてゆく宇宙的媒体である。場所とか時刻とかは、その変化の流れにおける相対的状況であるにすぎない。変化そのものは捉うべからざるものであって、ただ導くことができるだけである。

空間の中の流動は掴まえることはできずに、方向性を与えることができるだけである。こうした広大な考え方は、しかし日本建築において、人を圧倒するような大きなスケールのものとしてではなく、むしろ小さな、人体的なスケールの問題への関心として現われ、それが連続しながら、より大きな全体へとかかわってゆく過程として展開することとなった。相互関係の連続性──時間と空間の中を人間が動いてゆくときの秩序ある過程ということが強調点となった。建築は手近かな、かつ具体的なものから、遠く遥かな捉えがたいものへのリズミカルな発展によって、この空間的-時間的連続性への個人的かかわりあいを限定するものとなる。

日本建築において、この三次元的諸関係の展開は、無限の展開可能性を感じさせる非対称的秩序によってなされることになる。この秩序にもとづきながら、日本建築はその構造骨組の内外で、連続的な空間の特定部分を明確に限定する一連の面、ないし型（パターン）として展開してゆくのである。

105

Space is made manifest by rhythmic progressions that create a sense of movement and by the tensioned relationships of defining forms.

105

運動の感じをつくりだすリズミックな構成と、形を限定する緊張した相関関係とによって、空間は雄弁なものになる。

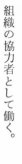

空間はそれの限定によって〝実在的〟（レアル）なものとなる。この空間構成の手がかりは
構造であり、構造はその本質的に幾何学的な秩序の含蓄と暗示のうちに姿をとる空間的な
組織の協力者として働く。

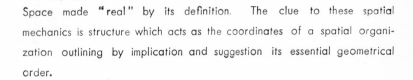

Space made "real" by its definition. The clue to these spatial
mechanics is structure which acts as the coordinates of a spatial organization outlining by implication and suggestion its essential geometrical
order.

110

114

116

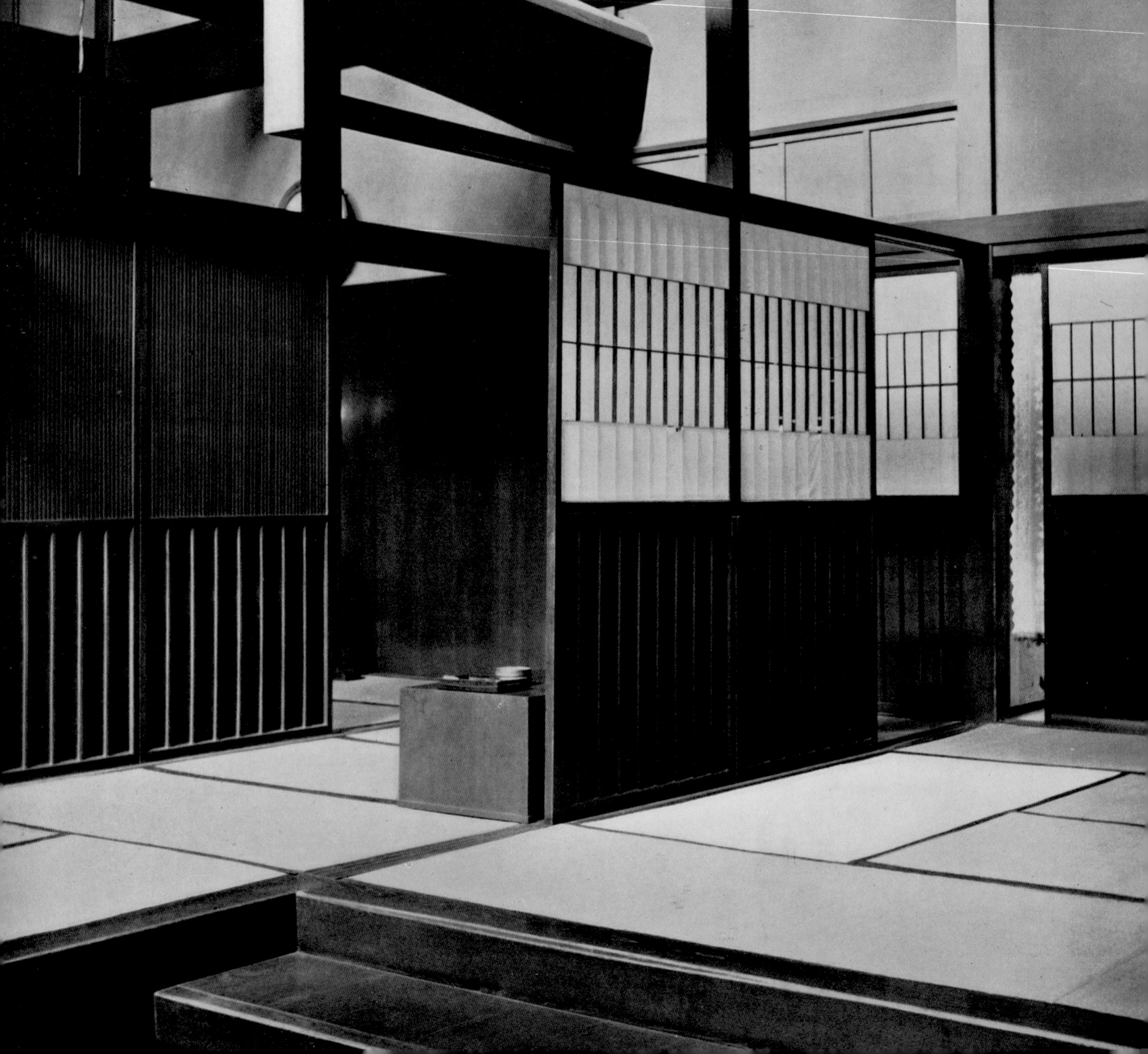

120

The meeting of architecture and nature was the key to spatial expression.   The building had a definite even precise relationship to the ground.   No exuberant interpenetration of the forms of nature and man.   The integral use of natural finishes and textures within the architecture made this gesture towards humanism redundant.   The expression of space as one and continuous was by the indication of ordered movement from interior to exterior.   The outward flow of asymmetrical rhythms from architecture —progressing from the stark geometry of the rectangle to the free and infinite rhythms of the rocks, the trees and the mountains.

122

150

建築と自然との出あいは空間的表現の焦点である。建物は大地に対して明確なというより決定的な関係をもっている。自然の形（フォーム）と人間との相関関係には、賑々しさは全くない。建築技術の範囲内での、自然のままの仕上げとテクスチュアの、まとまりのある使い方は、ヒューマニズムに対するこうした態度を豊かなものにする。一つであってしかも連続的な空間の表現は、内部から外部へ秩序ある動きを示すことによってつくりだされる。建築から外へ向う非対称的なリズムの流れ――矩形という鋭い幾何学的な構成から、石、樹木そして山々の、自由で無限定なリズムへの進み。

128

132

133

134

135

The linking rhythms occur far out in the gardens as occasional fine scale geometric patterns.

136

つながりあうリズムは、はるか庭のなか、偶然の、しかし微妙なスケールをもつ幾何学的な型（パターン）として再び現れる。

桂離宮、このユニィクな創作は、日本建築の傑作であり、日本建築がもっている諸性質を完ぺきにまで洗練したものである。日本建築の形と空間のあらゆる微妙な含蓄を、ひとつの統一された構想のうちにまとめたという意味で、桂は他のあらゆる建物よりもすぐれている。

緻密なセンスの持ち主であった桂の宮親王が建てられたこの離宮では、建築的体験がそのすべての面にわたって高められている。すなわち住まいの部分（御殿）のアブストラクトで簡素な高雅さや茶室（松琴亭など）の田舎風の単純さ、また広々した芝生と親しみのある庭、閑寂さから賑やかさへ、男性的なものから女性的なものへ、若々しい感じから老年の感じへ等々、ここには感受性の明確さおよび平衡と安静の感じがある。しかし桂の真の重要さは、建築的環境の内包的ならびに外延的な可能性に対して、近代人のこころをつよく覚醒させることのできた、おそらく最初のもので、それがあるということであろう。

The Katsura Palace, a unique creation, is Japanese architecture's masterpiece, the perfection of all its tendencies. It surpasses the other endeavors by gathering within a single unified concept the many subtle implications of Japanese form and space.

In this summer palace of a sensitive prince the full range of architectural experience is aroused: by the abstract and simple elegance of the living quarters and the rustic simplicity of the tea houses; by the expansive lawns and intimate gardens; from the cheerful to the lonely, from male to female, from yang to yin, there is clarity of sensation and a sense of balance and repose. But the real importance of Katsura is its capacity to awaken the modern mind, perhaps for the first time, to the intensive and extensive possibilities of an architectural environment.

138

166

140

非対称的にまとめられた黒と白の柄（パターン）が内から外へ続いている。

The continuity of the black and white asymmetrically ordered patterns from the exterior through the interior.

144

As one moves out from interior to exterior there is a sense of extension of architectural patterns into the landscape giving a space that is not merely formless and undifferentiated but is sharply defined, precise in its implied outlines, unique and yet at the same time "capable of unlimited extension" — of being a part of the whole.

145

建物の内から外へ動くにつれて、建築が庭園へ拡がっていくという感じがする。庭は、形のはっきりしていない、また分化していない空間ではなくて、輪廓の鋭くはっきりしている一つのユニークな空間となっているが、それと同時に、全体の一部分として〝無限に拡がってゆく可能性〟ももっている。

147

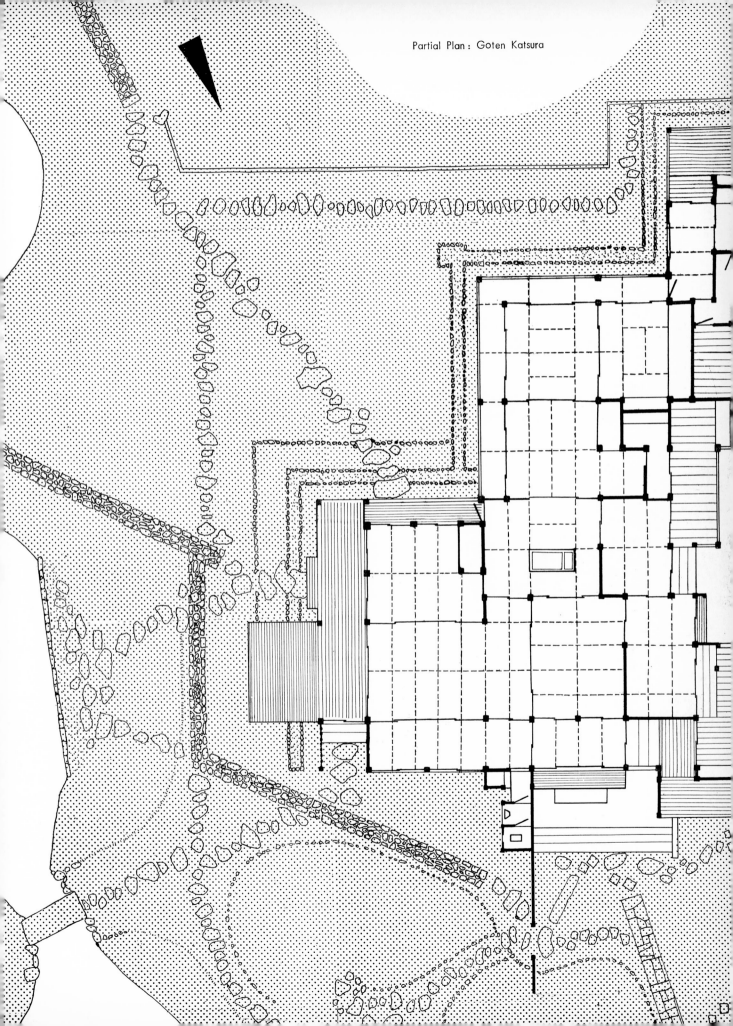

Partial Plan : Goten Katsura

There is no sense of a western formal heirarchy of space leading to a climax but rather a subtle movement from dark to light, from higher to lower, from manmade textures to natural textures...; a "working outward from precision toward the vague undefined void".

西洋建築の空間構成におけるごとき形式性の強い段階制（ヒエラルキー）へ導いてゆく（順々に進んで頂点へ導いてゆく）の感じではなくて、暗さから明るさへ、低いものから高いものへ、人工的なテクスチュアから自然なテクスチュアへの微妙な進行がある……〝明確なものから限定されないおぼろげな虚空への移りゆき〟。

桂の茶室・松琴亭は形式的的な厳格な感じが少く、より豊かで自然な構成をもって、御殿とはまた違った感じを表わしている。庭園と建物の結びつきは、建築的幾何学の庭園への延長であるというよりは、むしろ庭石の精緻な配置によって方向づけられる、リズミックな流れであるといいたい。

The Shokintei, tea pavilion of Katsura, expresses a different feeling—less formal and austere, richer and more natural in its patterns. The link with the landscape is not so much an extension of architectural geometry into the landscape as a rhythmic flow directed by the precise placement of the rocks of the garden.

151

建物の内部では、引込んだ面、出張った面の交錯が空間に区切りをつける。

In the interior the receding and advancing planes articulate space.

153

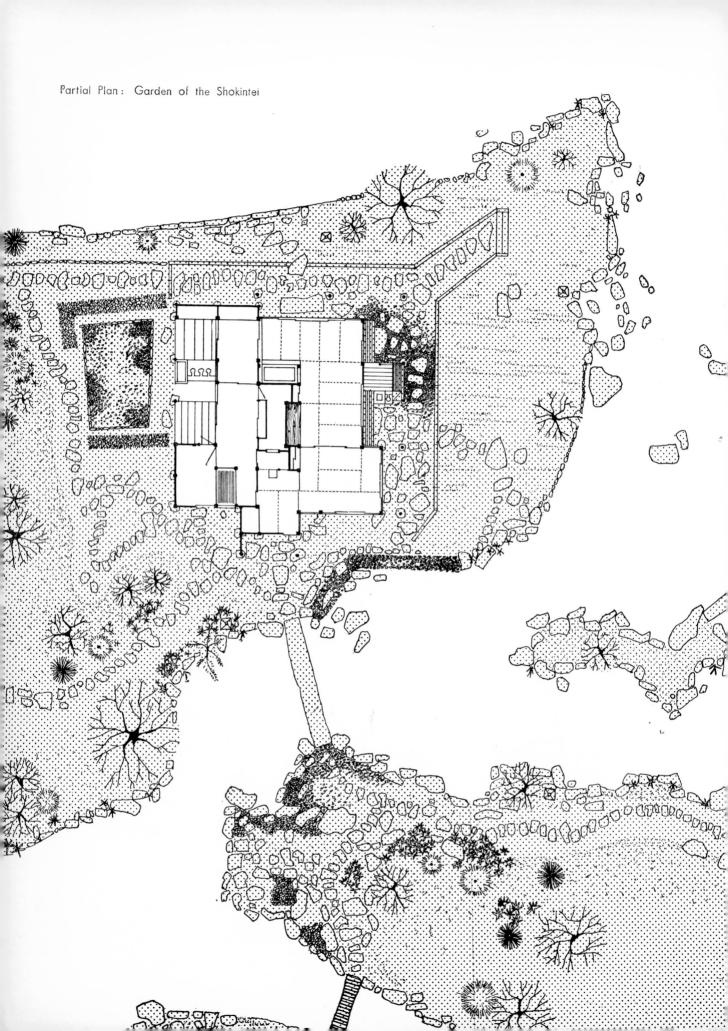

Partial Plan: Garden of the Shokintei

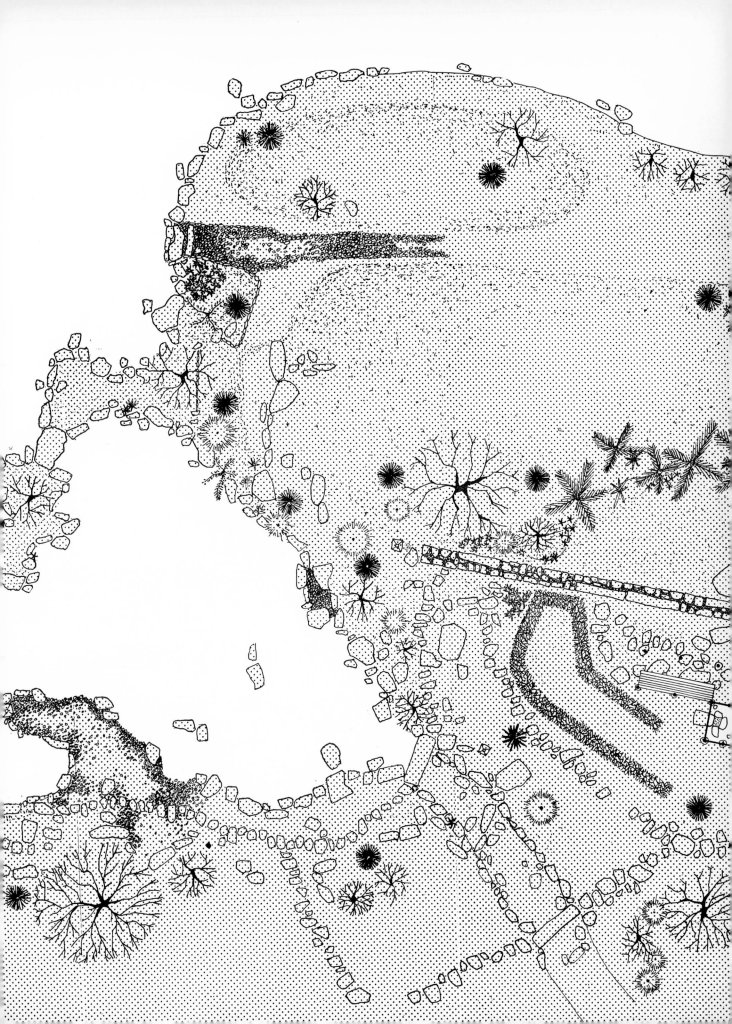

All relationships are abbreviated and subtle, encouraging the exercise of the imagination in grasping the whole.

156

◀ 158

庭は人間の宇宙に対する関係を完全に表現する……人間の実存の両分性（ディコトミー）……人間だけとしての、そしてまた宇宙の中の小さな一事物にすぎぬものとしての存在。この対照はスケールにおける外見上の矛盾によって表現される――庭には人体のスケールによる橋や小径があり、それらは歩いたり、渡ったりすることをひとに誘いかけるが、しかしそれと同時に山や島や海の、すなわち宇宙的空間の広大で永遠な眺めの感じをも与える、というのは、そこになんら時間に結びつけられた事物がないからである……。"身近かなもの、はっきりとして手でつかめるものに対する人間的なわれわれの執着は、はるかなもの、おぼろげなもの、無常なもの等の偉大な真実性を想いだすことによってのみ和らげられるものである。"

The garden expresses perfectly the relation of man to his universe ..... the dichotomy of man's existence   man alone and man in the world.   This contrast in scope is expressed by a seeming inconsistency of scale — for the garden contains elements of human scale : bridges and walks that invite participation and wandering yet at the same time by the absence of any time bound object it conveys a feeling of vast timeless vistas of mountains, islands and the sea — the universal space ..... " our mortal desire for the near, the precise, the closely seen, can be assuaged only by a reminder of the greater reality of the far, the vague, the dimly seen, the transient......".

Note   The suffixes "jinja", "jingu", and "gu" denote Shinto shrines, while the suffixes "ji", "in" denote Buddhist temples, all photographs taken with Rolleiflex camera.

図 版 説 明